Making Twig Mosaic Rustic Furniture

Larry Hawkins

Text written with and photography
by Douglas Congdon-Martin

77 Lower Valley Road, Atglen, PA 19310 USA

Printed in China
ISBN: 0-7643-0242-6

Published by Schiffer Publishing Ltd.
77 Lower Valley Road
Atglen, PA 19310
Please write for a free catalog.
This book may be purchased from the publisher.
Please include $2.95 for shipping.
Try your bookstore first.

We are interested in hearing from authors
with book ideas on related subjects.

Contents

Introduction

It was love at first sight! Poring over books about the rustic furniture tradition, my eye fell upon a wonderful piece of mosaic twig furniture, and I was hooked. The textures and colors were used in patterns that were at the same time intricate and simple. Generally the patterns were symmetrical, giving the work a sense of order and completeness. But then there is the surprise...a flash of color, a twig going off at a daring angle, a startlingly patterned bit of bark. Twig mosaic work has a sense of life and movement to it that keeps it from ever being ho-hum or commonplace. The medium and the form combine to make every piece unique, with its own personality and statement.

The origins of twig mosaic furniture are lost in history, but Ralph Kylloe traces it to England, France, Yugoslavia and other areas of Europe (*Rustic Traditions,* p. 14). Craig Gilborn cites a reference from an English magazine, *The Gardiner's Magazine,* in 1834 describing mosaic twig work: "The pieces are nailed to any flat surface of wood and very beautiful and elaborate patterns may be produced by arranging the pieces according to their sizes and the various colors of the bark." (Gilborn, *Adirondack Furniture,* p. 201) He goes on to suggest that the style may have been invented in England, where rustic was a common feature of the English garden (Gilborn, p. 203) in the late 18th and early 19th centuries. By 1834 surfaces of garden shelters were also being covered with mosaic patterns of twigs.

In America the art of mosaic twig flourished in the Adirondack region of New York. In this beautiful land of lakes and mountains people established get away homes and lodges for sports activities. This summer dwellings were usually of rustic design built by local craftsmen from local materials. These same craftsmen made much of the furniture for the lodges. Using twigs and bark they formed primitive yet elegant tables, chairs, beds, bureaus, sideboards and more. Whatever furnishing was needed, a clever woodworker could produce. The building of rustic furniture usually occupied the winter months, when their normal work, construction, lumbering, and other outdoor work was at a low ebb.

Gilborn calls mosaic twig work "the nineteenth century's main contribution to rustic art." (Gilborn, p. 30) The work was centered around Raquette Lake, New York, and spread to the surrounding communities of Mountain Lake, Long Lake, Brandreth Lake, Forked Lake, Mohegan Lake, Sagamore Lake, and Kora Lake. (Gilborn, p. 201) It graced the common rooms and guest rooms of some of the great lodges that thrived in the region during the latter part of the 19th century.

Rustic furniture is still treasured in the Adirondacks and is of growing interest to collectors and designers around the world, and among the most highly treasured forms is mosaic twig work. One of the greatest collections can be found at the Adirondack Museum at Blue Mountain Lake. Not only do they have historical pieces on display to the public, but each fall the craftspeople who are carrying on the tradition of rustic furniture gather at the museum to display and sell their arts.

One of the reasons I love mosaic twig work, in addition to its innate beauty and endless variety, is that it is so accessible. The raw materials are right outside my door and the tools are simple and inexpensive. All that remains is the ability to see the possibilities and to carry out a vision.

I hope you find this as enjoyable as I have and that this book will be of assistance in getting you started.

Materials

For almost everything I make I use hardwood cases as a base. They give the piece a solidity and weight that feels right. A good quality plywood may be substituted, and I do use plywood for very wide pieces like a headboard of a bed.

I go out and harvest twigs every few days. Because insects quickly attack dead wood, I use only live trees and branches. To avoid warping I let the wood age for 6 months before using it. I store it in a dry garage, standing it upright in bundles. I frankly do not know exactly what trees I use, picking them for color and texture rather than for their pedigree. I do, however, avoid birch, which tends to disintegrate over time. The birch bark, however, is quite durable and beautiful as an accent. Birch bark is traditionally used to fill spaces in twig work, though in this particular project I do not. That will have to wait for a future volume.

The twigs are nailed to the wood with brads. They need to be long enough to secure the twig. Because I do so many, I use a compressed air gun to drive my brads. A hammer and nailset will do as well, though it will be slower.

The finish should bring out the texture and color of the twigs, not conceal them. I use Danish oil, but a polyurethane could be used as well

The Twigs

The twigs I use are gathered in the woods. Because dead wood is subject to insects and the bark is likely to decay, I need to find live wood for my twigs. The bark, of course, is what gives color and life to the pieces I make. I look for four things: color, texture, shape and the quality of the bark. These three pieces are all maple, but they show a great degree of variation.

Silver birch has a wonderful bark, but is quite fragile, so I tend not to use it.

Wild cherry has a glossy, figured bark that gives a very nice effect.

Sometimes the trunk of the tree is unusable, but the branches are great, as in this unknown variety. This particular bark fades to a yellow in ultraviolet light, so I have to be careful where I use it. My horticulturist friends are shocked that I don't know all the varieties of the wood I use. Of course, the reason is that I am looking at the wood with very different eyes, and really care more about the look than the identity.

Sometimes the same bush will generate very different looking branches. These two are both from a tree known both as a red willow and a red twig dogwood. My apologies again to the horticulturists among you.

Bushes and shrubs also are good sources for twig variety. This is from a flowering bush near my Michigan home.

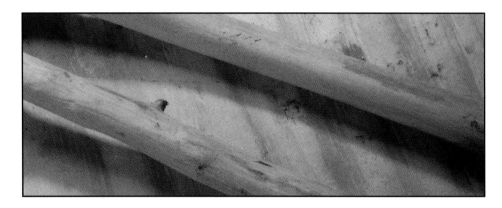

Sometimes I use the twigs stripped of their bark for a lighter effect. At the top is a twig of maple and below it a twig of cherry.

I keep a large and varied supply of twigs on hand. As in marquetry, it is the variety of color, texture, and size that makes Adirondack twigged furniture interesting. The twigs need to dry for six months before I use them.

The Project

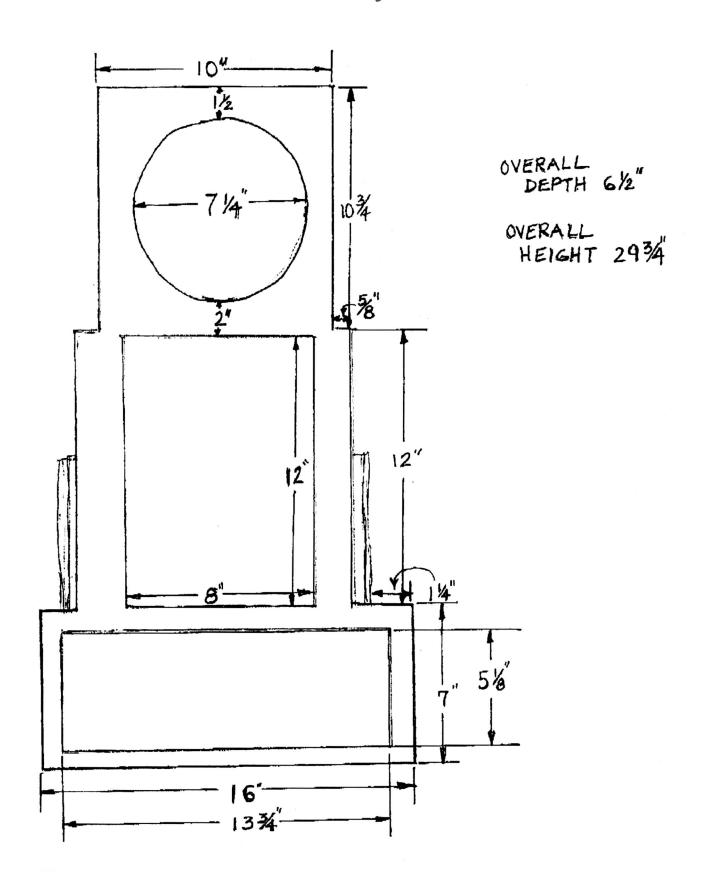

OVERALL DEPTH 6½"

OVERALL HEIGHT 29¾"

The wood is painted black so that if gaps develop between the twigs the background will not show.

The case pieces I make are of simple construction, using hard woods. This is a stepped clock with a drawer at the bottom and a cupboard in the center section.

From the back you can see the space left for the quartz movement of the clock. The beauty of twig work is that you can apply it to almost any piece of case work furniture, as you will see in the gallery. While I make all of my own furniture now, the first piece of twig furniture I made used an armoire from K-Mart. It is still a beautiful piece and can be seen in the gallery too.

8

To prepare the twigs, I begin by locating a straight section of the needed length...

Then, returning to the saw, I cut the twig to length.

And cut off the end.

The resulting twig is pretty straight. I need to decide where to cut the twig in half. I like to have some blemishes for a natural look, but not too many. At the end of this segment there are two blemishes. I will cut through this one, which will eliminate it, leaving the other for character.

I measure the length I will need for the piece I am covering, and add a little bit for safety.

Although I have tried splitting the twigs, I found it to be a less than satisfactory way of doing it. The bandsaw works much better. Eyeball the cut running the blade down the center of the twig.

Keep your fingers to the side for support, and situate your thumbs so they are safely out of the path of the blade.

After the bandsaw, I move to the belt sander. This will get rid of the ridges left by the saw, and make the surface much smoother. It also can be used to create flat parallel edges for good joining. Sand the flat surface first.

This creates a nice flat surface for attaching to the piece...

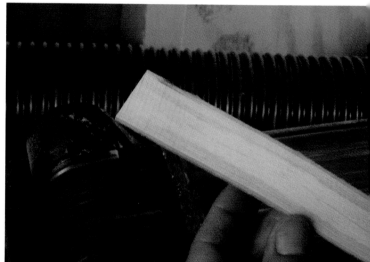

Sand until the saw marks are removed. Here you can see there is a little more to do.

and two nice, decorative surfaces.

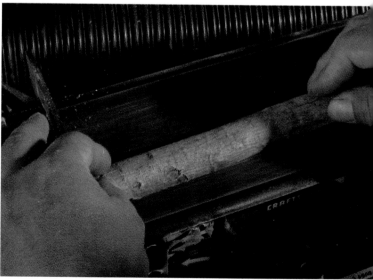

Continue...

until it is completely sanded.

The result is a surface that will join snugly against its adjoining twig.

Here you can see the difference between a sanded and an unsanded surface.

Do the other side in the same way. You want this to be parallel to the first side.

When the flat surface is finished sand one edge.

Finished.

11

Next hit the ends on a disc sander, keeping them perpendicular to the side edges.

Align the twig on the case piece so that one end and one edge are flush.

Go back to the belt sander to get rid of the burr.

Under the overhang...

I don't want the sides to be too thick. If they are I go back and reduce the bottom surface on the belt sander.

and mark the length...

12

Trim it to size. This can be done on the band saw...

and alignment. If either of these are wrong, make adjustments before proceeding. Small errors get multiplied as you add twigs.

or the disc sander.

There are two ways to attach the twigs. Both use wire brads that go 3/8" to 1/2" into the wood of the case.

Put the twig back on the piece and check for length...

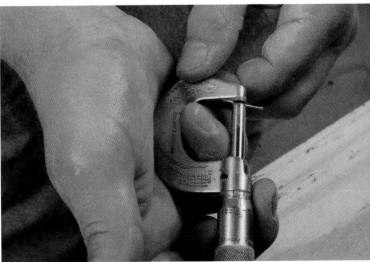

The traditional way is to use a wire brad. To avoid splitting the wood I drill a pilot hole through the twig, slightly smaller than the brad. Being an old machinist I measure the brad...

and the drill bit to be sure the drill bit is smaller.

and the other, with two spaced between.

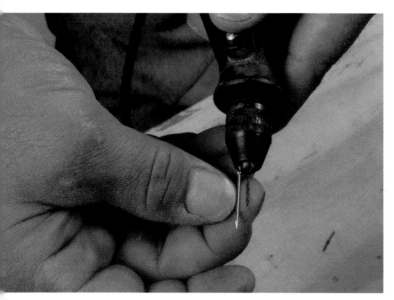

Set the drill bit in the chuck so the exposed portion is not as long as the brad.

Drive the brad in place.

This piece is on the bottom edge of the clock, so I want to be sure it is secure. It is about six inches long, so I will use four brads. Pieces higher up the cabinet, which take less abuse, will do nicely with two. Drill holes at one end

Knock them into place with a nail punch. Remember this is one half of a split twig. I am saving the matching half for the corresponding horizontal piece on the other side of the clock. I do this whenever possible to preserve the symmetry of the work.

The next piece I will do goes up the edges of the lower side panel of the clock. I measure it by laying the wood in place and marking. This is cut on the bandsaw as before.

If there are larger branch stubs as here, I knock them off with the bandsaw...

making the surface flat.

Then I make my splitting cut right through the flattened stub.

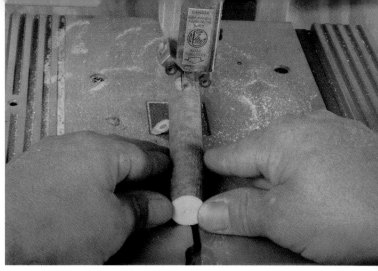

The two halves that twig will make the side pieces for this panel. This time I will attach them with a brad nailer. I use either an electric nailer or a pneumatic one. I prefer the pneumatic nailer for ease of use and low incidence of breakdown. As before make sure the brad goes from 3/8" to 1/2" into the case by holding the brad against the work.

Nail the twig in place. Whenever possible, don't put the nail right on the end of the twig. This will cause splitting. Instead begin nailing about 1/2" from the end. On these pieces I only need to use two brads.

Sometimes a twig will have a slight bend to it, as this one does.

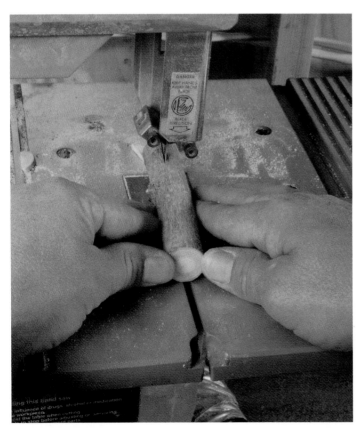

When that happens, hold the twig on the saw table so you can see the bend and cut a straight line down the middle. This effectively eliminates the bend.

You are always going to get some gaps, but the object is to get the wood as tight as possible. To do this, apply pressure with the thumb of the free hand while nailing.

The bottom panel is covered in what is called the "log cabin" pattern.

At this point in the pattern I am down to the last two pieces, so I need a twig that will be wide enough to fill the space when split.

For these tight fits it is often necessary to fine tune the twig with the sander.

The first panel complete.

I do the opposite panel next. This helps keep things even, and uses set-aside pieces before they get lost or used somewhere else. Begin with the bottom horizontal piece, set aside earlier, which is the mate to the other side's. The pattern on this panel matches its opposite.

I usually design my twigging patterns as I go. Here at the first shelf I could lay two twigs flat on the shelf...

and building the next segment up from there. This would give a nice effect.

Alternatively I could cover the next vertical panel and add a single, wider twig for the shelf. This is the option I will choose.

Test fit the twigs for the panel.

Make any necessary adjustments.

18

With the straight pattern of this panel, I usually get everything pretty much set before doing any nailing.

When the width is set, one at a time, adjust the lengths of the twigs and nail them in place.

For the shelf I could use one large twig or two smaller ones. The smaller size is more graceful, so that is what I choose. I want to leave the rounds of the bottom panel twigs exposed.

A twig for the front and back edges of the second panel...

The third panel of the side will repeat the log cabin pattern of the first. Begin with the bottom horizontal twig and follow with the side twigs and the others in the same order as the first panel.

and the panel of the second tier is complete.

Add the shelf...

Repeat on the other side. I try to match the vertical twigs for width as much as possible.

and the third panel is complete.

Repeat on the other side.

I have no firm design planned as I start the top panel, but I know it needs to be framed as a first step. I begin with shelf and the lower horizontal piece.

Continue with the top...

and the sides.

With the frame in place I'm going to use a variation of the log cabin pattern used before. I begin with horizontal pieces in the top and bottom of the frame.

Continue with two vertical members.

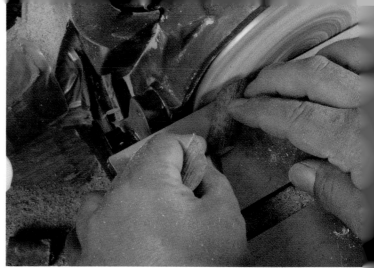

The diagonal members are ground to parallel 45 degree angles at their ends...

for this result.

Now at the corners I am going to run a diagonal member to create a long diamond in the center.

They fit together to create the top of the diamond.

Repeat at the bottom.

To fill the small corners outside of the diamond, I can either use two small twigs or one large one. Aesthetically I usually like the smaller twigs, but the tiny piece that ends up in the corner is unstable and hard to handle, so I think I'll use the one big piece this time.

Progress.

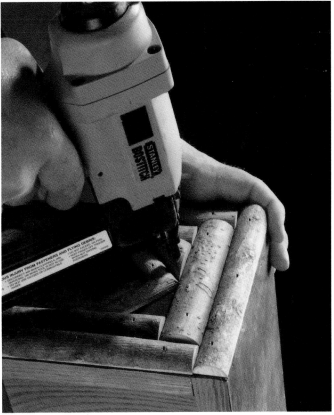

Grind the piece to fit and nail it in place.

Progress. Bring the other side up to this point before continuing.

I want to create an hourglass shape inside the center of the diamond. I begin by cutting a twig to the length of the long side.

Measure the half the length of the twig and mark one edge.

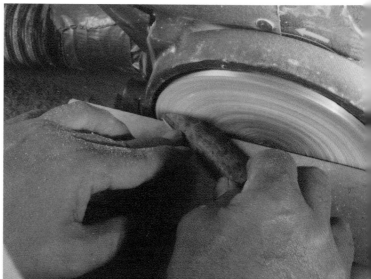

Grind from the corner of one edge to the center of the other, first from one corner...

then from the other.

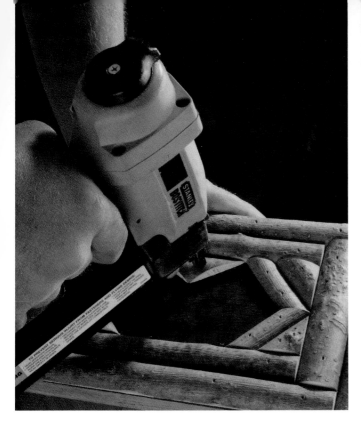

Nail one piece in place, then grind the other.

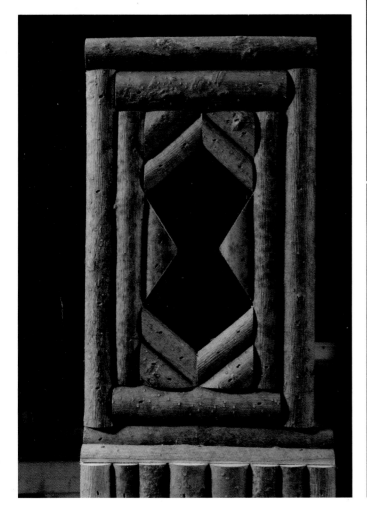

When both are in place this is the result.

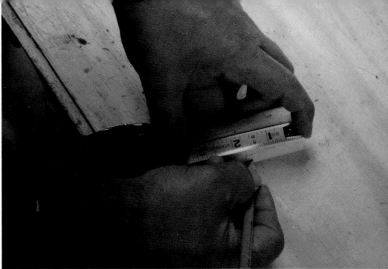

The spaces in the hour glass are filled with various colors of wood. In the top section I use a piece of stripped light wood. It is wide enough to fill the top quarter, so I mark the center

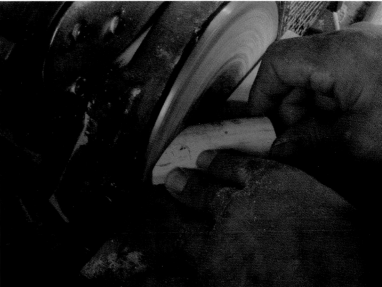

and grind down to the opposite corners.

With minor adjustments it fits like this.

A darker wood fills the next section in top and bottom....

Use the light, stripped wood for the bottom quarter in the same way.

and two twigs fill the center

26

for this result.

The knobs for the door and drawer are from a 1" diameter twig. I begin by cutting 1-1/2" lengths.

Slightly bevel the top edge off on the belt...

Use the sanding disc to remove the bark and trim the wood about 1/2" up from the base of the knob.

then smooth the surface.

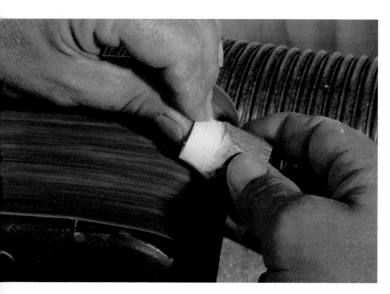

Move to the curved end of the sanding belt and refine this surface, giving it a concave surface.

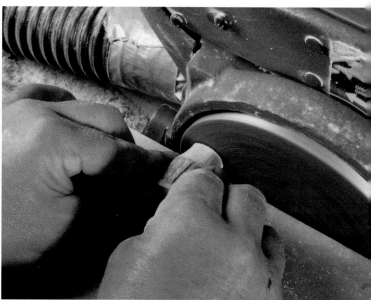

Flatten the base on the disc.

The result. By the way, I remove the door before continuing with the handles and the twigs.

Mark the position of the knobs on the drawer, about 2-1/2" in from the edges...

Because the drawer is so shallow, I am using a dowel to hold the knobs in place. I drill the appropriate sized hole in the knobs....

and 2" down.

and glue the dowels in place.

Drill a hole in position. You may or may not go all the way through.

Glue the handles in place and put the drawer aside to cure.

Make a starter hole in the knob and fill it with glue.

The knob of the door will be screwed in place. The hole is about half way down the door and 1" from the edge. I drill a hole from the front without going all the way down to the countersink.

Screw the knob in place, and set the door aside.

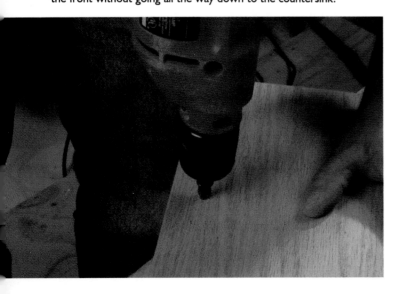

From the back I drill all the way down, creating a countersunk hole for the screw head.

The front of the cabinet begins with framing. Begin with the bottom horizontal piece, cutting it to be just as wide as the case, and thin enough so it doesn't overlap the board thickness beneath.

Move up to the next horizontal piece and do the same. When it is fitted, nail it in place. I try to put the nails on the lower edge of the twig so the nail hole doesn't show.

Continue by nailing the bottom twig in place. Remember it is important that these framing twigs do not overlap the drawer or door openings or hang below the cabinet.

Cut the vertical side pieces of the lower segment and nail in place.

The lower segment framed.

The vertical members of the second segment's frame use two twigs each. I using matching halves for the inside pair first.

Cut and fit the horizontal piece at the top of the second segment so it is just as wide as the case, but does not overlap the exposed twig ends.

Another matching pair makes the outside of the frame. I have used a different wood than on the inside pair, and have elected pieces that have matching branch cut-off to add some character.

Progress.

Continue framing with the horizontal piece above the top segment.

Add the vertical members.

Adjust the clock face where you want it...

Mark the position of the twelve...

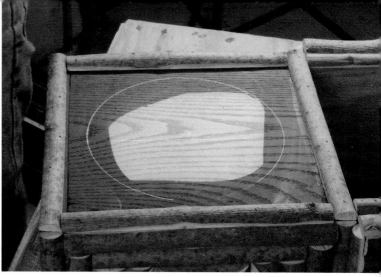

Ready to proceed.

and draw the outline of the clock face.

Drill the center hole.

Mark the center of the face.

The quartz movements come with various lengths of steams. The brass thread needs to emerge about 1/4" out of the wood.

Carefully attach the clock face to the wood. The glass lens of these clock faces are usually quite fragile. Be sure it does not open too much. The first round of nails I do not drive all the way home. This allows me to fix mistakes.

Install the movement...

When I am sure everything is fine, I finish the nailing.

and the hands.

Ready for twigging.

When the corner is fitted, mark the bezel on the other end.

Begin the twig work around the bezel with the corner pieces. I am bringing a piece out from the bezel into the corner.

A touch at the end of the belt sander...

will give me the curve I need to go around the bezel. Be careful. With this type of grinding, the wood tends to flick off of the sander, moving your fingers into it.

I begin to fill the spaces around the bezel, by adding a long, thin twig down the vertical side.

When all four corners are fitted, nail them in place.

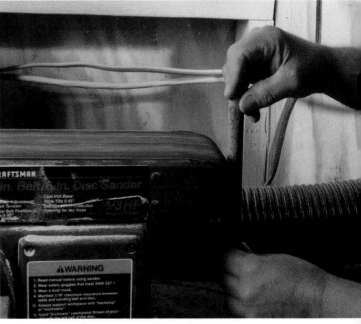

On the piece for the hinge side, you will need to use the end of the belt sander to create room for the hinge.

The result is a nice fit with room to allow the glass to be opened.

The spaces that are left offer the challenge of the curve of the bezel.

Continue with pieces at the top and bottom of the bezel.

Start by cutting a twig of the correct width to length.

Make the angled end on the sanding disc.

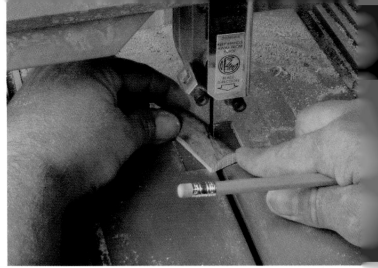

Cut outside the line on the band saw

Hold it in place...

and round the curve at the end of the sanding belt.

and draw the curve of the bezel.

Test fit and adjust....

until it is just right. Then nail it in place.

Continue the same process around the bezel.

The result.

Nature doesn't have a lot of long straight lines, which means that as a general principle I try to shorten long lines. Here on the top I do it by adding pieces to either end before filling the middle.

and long pieces...

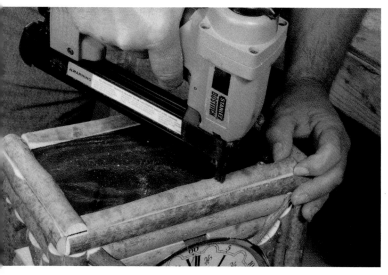

Next add twigs to the outside edges of the length.

working my way to the center.

I will continue to make the log cabin pattern adding short pieces...

The case piece is now complete. This is a good point to mention another consideration in twig choice. On a flat surface like this top, it is important that all the twigs be relatively the same depth. A flatter or thicker piece will look out of place and awkward.

Following the same principle of shortening the lengths, I cut end pieces for the drawer front....

Continue a second row in using the log cabin pattern. Begin with the end pieces...

and nail them in place.

and add the lengths. The top length should pretty much fill the space above the knobs.

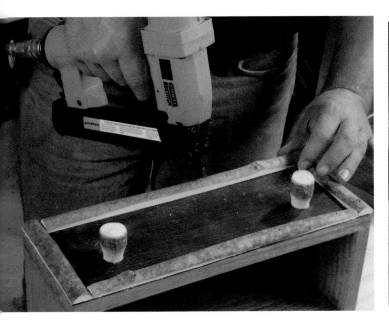

Add the long pieces of the frame.

Vertical twigs will fill most of the remaining surface. The twigs around the knobs will have to be shaped to fit.

Work your way from the sides toward the middle carrying the vertical twigs to about here.

Add a horizontal piece at the top and the bottom of the remaining space.

Carry smaller vertical pieces this far. I nail these small pieces with 5/8" brads.

To fill the remaining space I want to add a touch of color with green twigs.

There is a small gap at the top of the knob that needs to be filled.

I use a thin piece of wood and simply glue it in place.

The completed drawer front.

The door starts with the bottom edge.

Add the vertical framing twigs.

The design will have a pendulum-shaped center decoration. It will have a half inch wide twig coming down. I mark the top edge at the center and 1/4" on either side to allow for the pendulum arm.

The weight of the pendulum is a cross section of twig, about two inches in diameter. It is cut on the bandsaw and sanded. This piece is nicely spalted and should give some character to the clock.

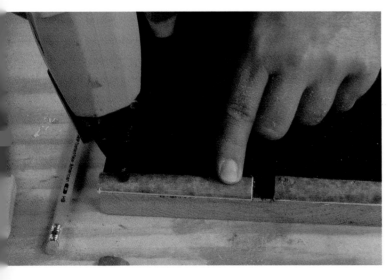

Divide the top framing twig so it leaves room for the pendulum arm.

The arm is a stripped twig, making it light also. I'm putting it at an angle to help define it as a pendulum. It also is a nice design element, going against the overall symmetry of the piece.

Apply glue to the weight...

Next is a horizontal piece at the bottom.

and put it at the end of the arm.

Vertical pieces are next. First one side...

I begin filling in the door starting with a horizontal piece at the top, cut to go around the pendulum arm.

then the other. This twig is in two pieces to work around the knob.

Continuing with the log cabin pattern, do the horizontal pieces, bottom and top. The top one is divided. I use the two halves of one twig to get the full width. Cut the twig for the length of the longer side, and trim the two sides from it.

One of the next two vertical pieces had to be ground slightly to go around the pendulum....

and the other to go around the knob.

The next horizontal piece at the bottom created a small place beside the pendulum that needs a carefully ground fill. It should look like the bottom end of the next vertical piece.

Mark where the vertical piece needs to be trimmed to accommodate the pendulum

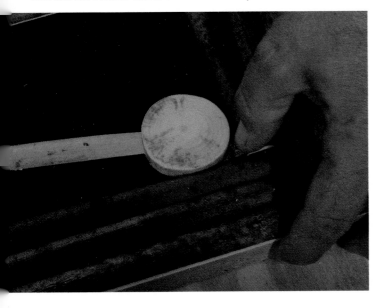

Apply glue and put it in place.

and cut and grind it to fit.

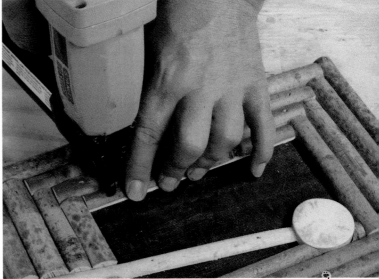

Add the next horizontal member, pieced around the pendulum arm.

Add the opposite vertical twig.

Do the horizontal twig in the same way...mark...

Continue the log cabin pattern. When you get to the tapering side of the pendulum, cut the twig to length...

and grind to fit.

and taper one side on the sanding belt to fit.

50

Remember, when working with these very small pieces, glue works better than nails.

The result.

Some green twig in the center adds color and unifies the door with the drawer.

Reattach the door.

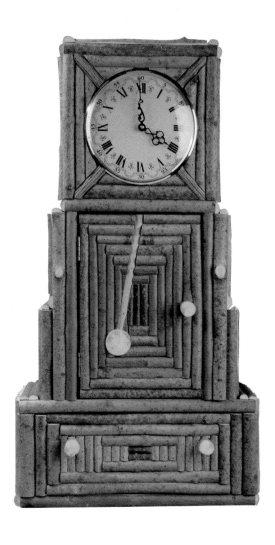

Ready for finishing.

I use a Danish oil finish for the clock. This brings out the natural color of the twigs and makes it come to life. Begin at the top.

Continue with the door.

Work carefully around the bezel.

The other nice thing that the finish does is bring out the differences in wood color like here on the upper side panel.

54

Gallery